Parental and Child anger: Anger Management Techniques And Child-building Up Tips For Parents

Alice D. Jackson

Table of contents

- **STOP STRUGGLING FOR POWER**
- **Give up these things**
- **What do I do instead?**

Chapter 5 9 child-building up tips can help you feel more fulfilled as a parent.

Introduction

Does it feel like you are always yelling at your child? Tired of being calm at one moment and angry at the next? Why couldn't he listen the first time? Or why are they always fighting and screaming? Or only if she just stops throwing all her toys, I wouldn't have to get angry. " Tons of techniques to control your child's behaviour can help you, but if you are unable to control your behaviour, that will be a bigger issue.

Instead of focusing on your kid's behaviour, let's have a look at what's bothering you.
When I thought of becoming a parent, I thought I must have understood this parenting thing thoroughly. I thought

that I would be the most patient, calm, loving mama who took it all in her stride and responded with compassion and empathy to her kids. If you're anything like me, you would have imagined what becoming a parent would be like: taking trips to parks, arts and crafts projects, pretend plays, bedtime stories, and things like that. Parenting triggers are not something you gave a thought about before becoming a parent, right? Sure, you knew that there would be difficulties and struggles, but you always pictured how you would handle them patiently and calmly.

What you might not have imagined was losing it when the toddler refuses to eat the food that you've lovingly prepared for them, the whining that starts just before you thought of relaxing while having a hot cup of coffee for yourself and a book to read, or siblings fighting over the TV remote to watch their favourite shows. Every parent has a skeleton in their parenting closet. We all get triggered! We all react, yell, shame, spank, and whatnot. We all get into situations where it just gets to us and we react in ways we never expected to behave.

Those are the toughest moments of our parenting journey where we start doubting ourselves as parents. These reactions to triggers challenge our self-perception and create a mismatch between what we believe as parents and how we behave, making the parenting journey more difficult.

Chapter 1

Helping Children Understand and Manage Anger

Children must have a foundation of basic cognitive processes before they are able to develop an understanding of anger. Three key components contribute to children's understanding of anger: memory, language, and self-regulatory behaviors.

Memory develops considerably during early childhood and allows children to recall aspects of anger-evoking interactions. Children often model what they have learned by watching adults and family members, including the expression of anger. When faced with anger-arousing emotions, they may recall strategies that they witnessed at an early age. If the anger management strategy was an unhelpful or aggressive one, children may need to be reminded of and given choices of more productive ways to handle their emotions.

Children gain an understanding of their feelings by talking about emotions. The development of language skills help children understand and label their emotions; therefore, children will have varying degrees in their ability to identify and label angry feelings. Parents and caregivers play an important role in the process of talking about emotions. Children learn to model a variety of approaches by listening to their parents and caregivers talk about emotions.

Emotion regulation provides children with the ability to monitor, evaluate, and modify their emotional reactions to anger in order to accomplish their goals. Self Regulatory behaviors allow children to control impulses and delay immediate gratification. Parents and caregivers can guide children in the development of strategies for understanding emotions associated with anger by modeling effective emotion regulation skills.

Effective Coping Strategies for Children

Children have different coping potentials, or in other words, the perceived ability to deal with an anger inducing event Parents and caregivers can engage children in a variety of strategies to assist with their feelings of anger. For best outcomes, include children in determining strategies and solutions.

Stop and think - Parents and caregivers can teach children to apply the thought stopping technique when faced with feelings of anger. By saying "stop" out loud or thinking it, children are given time to distract themselves from the event. Thinking of a positive or happy memory is also a useful approach when dealing with anger. Focusing on positive memories distracts children from the negative emotions that they are feeling

Do something physical - Engage children in an activity that uses their entire body such as jumping jacks, running, or dancing. Children can also refocus their anger by playing with play dough or modeling clay, which can be rolled, twisted, and pulled apart. Physical activities can help children refocus their anger while providing the necessary time to calm down.

Relax - Children often need to take a time-out to relax and regroup, and changing the environment that is causing feelings of anger can help. Parents and caregivers can have children read a story, take a relaxing bath, or draw and color a picture. By providing a calming and soothing alternative, children are able to relax and refocus

Talk to children - By expressing empathy and encouraging children to label their feelings, parents and caregivers can assist children in understanding their feelings of anger. Depending on the age of the child, it can also be helpful to have children draw a picture of what their anger looks like in order to help them express themselve.

Knowing when to seek help - It is normal for children to become upset from time to time, but parents and caregivers may find it beneficial to seek professional help. Some indicators for parents may include the struggle with ongoing and intense outbursts, leading to isolation of friends. If children are experiencing recurrent stomach aches or headaches due to the suppression of anger, professional help may also be advantageous

Children's anger can be stressful and frustrating for caregivers and children; but with understanding and employing a few helpful strategies, it is possible to help children to recognize and manage their anger effectively.

When You Get Angry At Your Child

Every parent gets angry at his or her children sometimes.

The pressures on parents are endless: health and financial worries, children fighting, just getting dinner on the table. In the middle of that stress, enter our child, who has awakened early and wants us up, or has suddenly remembered that she never did her assignment for school today, or is teasing her little brother. And we snap.

But no matter how aggravating we find our child's behavior, their behavior doesn't cause our angry response. If we're in a state of well-being, we can sometimes stay patient and empathic and settle the storm.

But if we're stressed, we're primed to over-react. We see our child's behavior ("He hit her again!"), and we draw a conclusion ("He's going to be a psychopath!") which triggers other conclusions ("I've failed as a parent!"). This cascade of thoughts creates a run-away train of emotions -- in this case fear, dismay, guilt. We can't bear those feelings. The best defense is a good offense, so we lash out at our child in anger. The whole process takes all of two seconds.

Your child may be pushing your buttons, but he isn't causing your response. Any issue that makes you feel like lashing out has roots in your own early years. We know this because we lose our ability to think clearly at those moments, and we start acting like children ourselves, throwing our own tantrums.

Don't worry. That's normal. We all enter the parenting relationship wounded in some way from our childhoods, and our kids surface all those wounds. We can expect our kids to act out in ways that send us over the cliff at times. That's why it's our responsibility as the grownup to stay away from the cliff.

Chapter 2

WHY We Get So Angry At Our Kids

Parents and kids have the ability to trigger each other as no one else can. Even as adults we are often irrational in relation to our own parents. (Who has greater power to annoy you and make you act childish than your own mother or father?)

Similarly, our kids push our buttons precisely because they are our children. Psychologists call this phenomenon "ghosts in the nursery," by which they mean that our children stimulate the intense feelings of our own childhoods, and we often respond by unconsciously re-enacting the past that's etched like forgotten hieroglyphics deep in our psyches. The fears and rage of childhood are powerful and can overwhelm us even as adults. It can be enormously challenging to lay these ghosts to rest.

It helps to know all this, if we're struggling to cope with anger. Just as important, because it gives us incentive to control ourselves, we need to know that parental anger can be harmful to young children.

What Happens to Your Child When You Scream or Hit ?
Imagine your husband or wife losing their temper and screaming at you. Now imagine them three times as big as you, towering over you. Imagine that you depend on that person completely for your food, shelter, safety, protection. Imagine they are

your primary source of love and self-confidence and information about the world, that you have nowhere else to turn. Now take whatever feelings you have summoned up and magnify them by a factor of 1000. That is something like what happens inside your child when you get angry at him.

Of course, all of us get angry at our children, even, sometimes, enraged. The challenge is to call on our maturity so that we control the expression of that anger, and therefore minimize its negative impact.

Anger is scary enough. Name calling or other verbal abuse, in which the parent speaks disrespectfully to the child, takes a higher personal toll, since the child is dependent on the parent for his very sense of self. And children who suffer physical violence, including spanking, have been proven to exhibit lasting negative effects that reach into every corner of their adult lives, from lowered IQ to stormier relationships to a higher likelihood of substance abuse.

If your young child does not seem afraid of your anger, it's an indication that he or she has seen too much of it and has developed defenses against it -- and against you. The unfortunate result is a child who is less likely to want to behave to please you, and is more open to the influences of the peer group That means you have some repair work to do. Whether or not they show it -- and the more often we get angry, the more defended they will be, and therefore less likely to show it --

our anger is nothing short of terrifying to our children.

How can you handle your own anger?

Since you're human, you'll sometimes find yourself in "fight or flight" mode, and your child will start to look like the enemy. When we're swept with anger, we're physically ready to fight. Hormones and neurotransmitters are flooding our bodies. They cause your muscles to tense, your pulse to race, your breathing to quicken. It's impossible to stay calm at those points, but we all know that clobbering our kids -- while it might bring instant relief -- isn't really what we want to do.

The most important thing to remember about anger is NOT to act while you're angry. You'll feel an urgent need to act, to teach your child a lesson. But that's your anger talking. It thinks this is an emergency. It almost never is, though. You can teach your child later, and it will be the lesson you actually want to teach. Your child isn't going anywhere. You know where she lives.

So commit now to No hitting, No swearing, No calling your child names, No meting out any punishment while angry. What about screaming? Never at your children, that's a tantrum. If you really need to scream, go into your car with the windows rolled up and scream where no one can hear, and don't use words, because those make you angrier. Just scream.

Your children get angry too, so it's a double gift to them to find constructive ways to deal with your anger: you not only don't hurt them, you offer them a role model. Your child will certainly see you angry from time to time, and how you handle those situations teaches children a lot.

Will you teach your child that might makes right? That parents have tantrums too? That screaming is how adults handle conflict? If so, they'll adopt these behaviors as a badge of how grown-up they are.

Or will you model for your child that anger is part of being human, and that learning to manage anger responsibly is part of becoming mature? Here's how.

1. Set limits BEFORE you get angry.

Often when we get angry at our children, it's because we haven't set a limit, and something is grating on us. The minute you start getting angry, it's a signal to do something. No, not yell. Intervene in a positive way to prevent more of whatever behavior is irritating you.

If your irritation is coming from you -- let's say you've just had a hard day, and their natural exuberance is wearing on you -- it can help to explain this to your children and ask them to be considerate and keep the behavior that's irritating you in check, at least for now.

If the children are doing something that is increasingly annoying -- playing a game in which someone is likely to get hurt, stalling when you've asked them to do something, squabbling while you're on the phone -- you may need to interrupt what you're doing, restate your expectation, and redirect them, to keep the situation, and your anger, from escalating.

2. Calm yourself down BEFORE you take action.

When you feel this angry, you need a way to calm down. Awareness will always help you harness your self-control and shift your physiology: Stop, Drop (your agenda, just for a minute), and Breathe. That deep breath is your pause button. It gives you a choice. Do you really want to get hijacked by those emotions?

Now, remind yourself that it isn't an emergency. Shake the tension out of your hands. Take ten more deep breaths.

You might try to find a way to laugh, which discharges the tension and shifts the mood. Even forcing yourself to smile sends a message to your nervous system that there's no emergency, and begins calming you down. If you need to make a noise, hum. It can help to physically discharge your rage, so you might try putting on some music and dancing.

If you can find 15 minutes a day for a mindfulness practice while kids are in school or napping, you can actually build the neural capacity so that it's easier to calm yourself in these moments of upset. But even daily life with children should give you plenty of opportunities to practice, and every time you do resist acting while you're angry, you rewire your brain so that you have more self control.

Some people still follow the timeworn advice to clobber a pillow, but it's best if you can do that kind of discharging in private, because watching you clobber that pillow can be pretty scary for your child. He knows perfectly well that the pillow is a stand-in for his head and the image of crazy hitting mommy will be seared into his memory. This is probably a questionable strategy anyway, because research suggests that hitting something -- anything -- confirms to your body that indeed this is an emergency and you should stay in "fight or flight." So it may "discharge" energy and wear you out, but it doesn't get to the feelings driving the anger and may actually make you more angry.

If you can instead breathe deeply and tolerate the angry feelings, you will probably notice that right under the anger is fear, sadness, disappointment. Let yourself feel those feelings by noticing the sensations they cause in your body. Don't reinforce them by "thinking" about why you're upset; just breathe into that tension in your body and watch it change and fade. The anger will melt away.

3. **Take Five.**

Recognize that an angry state is a terrible starting place to intervene in any situation. Instead, give yourself a timeout and come back when you're able to be calm. Move away from your child physically so you won't be tempted to reach out and touch him violently. Just say, as calmly as you can,

"I am too mad right now to talk about this. I am going to take a timeout and calm down."

Exiting does not let your child win. It impresses upon them just how serious the infraction is, and it models self-control. Use this time to calm yourself, not to work yourself into a further frenzy about how right you are.

If your child is old enough to be left for a moment, you can go into the bathroom, splash water on your face, and do some breathing. But if your child is young enough to feel abandoned when you leave, they will follow you screaming. (Even many adult partners will do this. Just saying.)

If you can't leave your child without escalating their upset, walk to the kitchen sink and run your hands under the water. Then, sit on the couch near your child for a few minutes, breathing deeply and saying a little mantra that restores your calm, like one of these:

"This is not an emergency."
"Kids need love most when they deserve it least."
"He's acting out because he needs my help with his big feelings."
"Only love today."
It's fine to say your mantra aloud. It's good role modeling for your kids to see you handle your big emotions responsibly. Don't be surprised if your child picks up your mantra and starts to use it when he's angry.

4. Listen to your anger, rather than acting on it.

Anger, like other feelings, is as much a given as our arms and legs. What we're responsible for is what we choose to do with it. Anger often has a valuable lesson for us, but acting while we're angry, except in rare situations requiring self-defense, is rarely constructive, because we make choices that we would never make from a rational state. The constructive way to handle anger is to limit our expression of it, and when we calm down, to use it diagnostically: what is so wrong in our life that we feel furious, and what do we need to do to change the situation?

Sometimes the answer is clearly related to our parenting: we need to enforce rules before things get out of hand, or start putting the children to bed half an hour earlier, or do some repair work on our relationship with our child so that she stops treating us rudely. Sometimes we're surprised to find that our anger is actually at our partner who is not acting as a full partner in parenting, or even at our boss. And sometimes the answer is that we're carrying around anger we don't understand that spills out onto our kids, and we need to seek help though counseling or a parents' support group.

5. Remember that "expressing" your anger to another person can reinforce and escalate it.
Despite the popular idea that we need to "express" our anger so that it doesn't eat away at us, there's nothing constructive about expressing anger "at" another person. Research shows that expressing anger while we are angry actually makes us more angry. This in turn makes the other person hurt and afraid, so they get more angry. Not surprisingly, instead of

solving anything, this deepens the rift in the relationship.

What's more, expressing anger isn't truly being authentic. Anger is an attack on the other person, because you feel so upset inside. True authenticity would be expressing the hurt or fear that's giving rise to the anger -- which you might do with a partner. But with your child, your job is to manage your own emotions, not to put them on your child, so you need to be more measured.

The answer is always to calm yourself first. Then consider what the deeper "message" of the anger is, before you make decisions about what to say and do.

6. **WAIT before disciplining.**

Make it a point NEVER to act while angry. Nothing says you have to issue edicts on the fly. Simply say something like:

"I can't believe you hit your brother after we've talked about how hitting hurts. I need to think about this, and we will talk about it this afternoon. Until then, I expect you to be on your best behavior."

Take a ten minute timeout to calm yourself. Don't rehash the situation in your mind -- that kind of stewing will always make you more angry. Instead, use the techniques above to calm yourself. But if you've taken a ten minute timeout and still don't feel calm enough to relate constructively, don't hesitate to put the discussion off:

"I want to think about what just happened, and we will talk about it later. In the meantime, I need to make dinner and you need to finish your homework, please."

After dinner, sit down with your child and, if necessary, set firm limits. But you will be more able to listen to his side of it, and to respond with reasonable, enforceable, respectful limits to his behavior.

7. **Avoid physical force, no matter what**.

85% of adolescents say they've been slapped or spanked by their parents (Journal of Psychopathology, 2007).

And yet study after study has proven that spanking and all other physical punishment has a negative impact on children's development that lasts throughout life. The American Academy of Pediatrics recommends strongly against it.

I personally wonder if the epidemic of anxiety and depression among adults in our culture is caused in part by the aftermath of so many of us having grown up with adults who hurt us. Many parents minimize the physical violence they suffered, because the emotional pain is too great to acknowledge. But repressing the pain suffered in childhood just makes us more likely to hit our own children.

Spanking may make you feel better temporarily because it discharges your rage, but it is bad for your child, and ultimately sabotages everything positive you do as a parent. Spanking, and even slapping, has a way of escalating. There's even some evidence that spanking is addictive for the parent, because it gives you a way to discharge that upset and feel better. But there are better ways for you to feel better, that don't hurt your child.

Do whatever you need to do to control yourself, including leaving the room. If you can't control yourself and end up resorting to physical force, apologize to your child, tell him that hitting is never ok, and get yourself some help.

8. Avoid threats.

Threats made while you're angry will always be unreasonable. Since threats are only effective if you are willing to follow through on them, they undermine your authority and make it less likely that your kids will follow the rules next time. Instead, tell your child that you need to think about an appropriate response to this infraction of the rules. The suspense will be worse than hearing a string of threats they know you won't enforce.

9. Monitor your tone and word choice.

Research shows that the more calmly we speak, the more calm we feel, and the more calmly others respond to us. Similarly, use of swear words or other highly charged words makes us and our listener more upset, and the situation escalates. We have the power to calm or upset ourselves and the person we are speaking with by our own tone of voice and choice of words. (Remember, you're the role model.)

10. **Still angry?**
Don't get attached to your anger. Once you've listened to it and made appropriate changes, let go of it. If that isn't working, remember that anger is always a defense. It shields us from feeling vulnerable.

To get rid of anger, look at the hurt or fear under the anger. Maybe your son's tantrums scare you, or your daughter's so obsessed with her friends that she's dismissive of the family, which hurts you. Once you accept those underlying emotions and let yourself feel them, your anger will dissipate. And you'll be more able to intervene constructively with your child to solve what seemed like an insurmountable problem.

11. **Make and post a list of acceptable ways to handle anger.** Sometime when things at your house are calm, talk to your kids about acceptable ways to handle anger. Is it ever okay to hit someone? Is it okay to throw things? Is it okay to yell? Remember that since you're the role model, the rules that apply to your child also apply to you.

Then, make a list together of acceptable ways to handle anger, and post it on your refrigerator where everyone in the family can read it regularly. Let your kids see you check it as you start to get mad.

"Tell the other person what you want without attacking them."
"Put on music and dance out your angries.
"When you want to hit, clap your hands around your own body and hold yourself."

12. **Choose your battles.**

Every negative interaction with your child uses up valuable relationship capital. Focus on what matters, such as the way your child treats other humans. In the larger scheme of things, his jacket on the floor may drive you crazy, but it isn't worth putting your relationship bank account in the red over. Remember that the more positive and connected your relationship with your child is, the more likely he is to follow your direction.

13. **Consider that you're part of the problem.**

If you're open to emotional growth, your child will always show you where you need to work on yourself. If you're not, it's hard to be a peaceful parent, because everything will trigger you to act your worst. In every interaction with our child, we have the power to calm or escalate the situation. Your child may be acting in ways that aggravate you, but you are not a helpless victim.

Take responsibility to manage your own emotions first. Your child may not become a little angel overnight, but you'll be amazed to see how much less angry your child acts once you learn to stay calm in the face of her anger.

14. **Keep looking for effective ways to discipline that encourage better behavior.**

There are hugely more effective ways to discipline than anger, and, in fact, research shows that disciplining with anger sets up a cycle that encourages misbehavior.

Some parents are surprised to hear that there are families where children are never punished, even with consequences or timeouts, and parental yelling is infrequent. Limits are set, of course, and there are expectations for behavior, but these are enforced through the parent-child connection and by helping children with the needs and upsets that drive their "bad" behavior. The research is clear that these families produce children who are more emotionally intelligent and thus more able to manage their behavior.

15. **If you frequently struggle with your anger, seek counseling.**
There's no shame in asking for help. The shame is in reneging on your responsibility as a parent by damaging your child physically or psychologically.

Chapter 3

How to identify Parenting triggers

What are the parenting triggers?

Parenting Triggers are the ones that are caused by our child's behaviour. Sometimes, when they say, do, or feel something and we have an automatic negative response in return, we yell, lash out, shut down, cry, try to escape, or sometimes you feel compelled to punish or shame your children when they feel triggered. We may say or do things that we normally wouldn't and feel guilty about it later.

A trigger can be anything when you experience the present moment that activates the feeling from the past. We may act in a way that's not in keeping with the present. A trigger often activates an old wound from our childhood, like not being heard, respected, or taken for granted. Many times, when our children get upset, we get angry or annoyed by their way of expressing certain feelings (whining, tantrums, or crying). It's more often about ourselves than our difficulties in processing these emotions than the child's behaviour.

Triggers cause us to act in a certain way that, as parents, we do not value and believe. Our responses when triggered are usually extreme, and we feel lost, angry, and out of control. They are almost automatic and sometimes out of proportion too, and it is hard to understand why. They are often related to the experiences we get from our childhood, upbringing, or schooling.

Triggers don't always have to be something negative. Our children have done it too. Sometimes it can be a positive experience our child is having that we have never had a chance to trigger in us. Many of us were not "allowed" freedom or independence. We were never free from unnecessary control. So sometimes our children's living this way can trigger us.
The most important part of parenting with a trigger is that you are not reacting to your child's certain ways of behaving, but you are having a reaction because of what that behaviour means to you and that is triggered by your past experiences.

What does a parenting trigger look like?

We all have different triggers, but our children experiencing strong emotions is a huge trigger for many of us. It is often because we were raised in an environment where we were not free to express our emotions safely. If we do so, then it would lead to us being punished, shamed, ignored, or otherwise invalidated. So, when our children go through those emotions, we often feel threatened or overwhelmed by them, or simply do not know how to deal with them because no one ever modelled them for us as children. Even children being "silly" can sometimes bring us back to our inner child who was shamed for being silly. Emotions can be very powerful as a trigger. But I can assure you that this gets easier with time and support.

For many of us, it was punishable to disobey as a child, so when our children do, we often feel confronted and challenged. And it invokes a reactionary response based on what happened to us. Sometimes we get triggered because the things our children do are the things we would have been punished, belittled, shamed, or bullied for. We feel protective and fear they will experience the same things. We have to keep reminding ourselves that our job isn't to stop them from being themselves, but rather to show them that they are unconditionally loved and appreciated for being their authentic selves. We should not unintentionally recreate our fears by stopping them from being themselves. We should advocate for them when people around them aren't respectful.

In some cases, we are triggered when we do not know what to do in that situation because we are not parenting as we are trying to parent, and situations like these can make us feel like it's a lot. I know when I sometimes have moments like these when my daughter is struggling and I do not know what to do to help her and I get triggered into feeling worthless and helpless.

Triggers are as varied as we are as parents. Here are some common parenting triggers that I have heard and experienced:

- *Concerns about wasting food.*
- *Concerns about a child not eating enough and worried about health.*
- *Concerns about child's safety.*
- *When children are being authentically themselves.*
- *Children crying.*
- *When children don't share.*
- *Child is unkind.*
- *Children being dishonest.*
- *Children are not using manners.*
- *When Children talk back.*
- *Children being picky.*
- *Children being "bossy".*
- *Behaving rudely.*
- *Being angry.*
- *Children throwing a tantrum.*
- *Children being silly.*
- *Child not listening to you.*

- *Child not taking you seriously.*
- *Loud Noises.*
- *Mess*
- *Lack of privacy.*
- *Lack of personal space.*
- *Feeling unappreciated.*
- *Feeling ignored.*
- *Feeling unheard.*
- *Feeling touched out.*
- *Feeling disrespected.*
- *Feeling tired.*
- *Feeling overwhelmed.*

Many of these are related to feelings and emotions that cause triggers. These triggers can steal the moment from being able to be the parent you want to be. We act impulsively in a protective way to stop our emotional discomfort instead of what we genuinely want for our child.

Some of these things help us respectfully teach our children to navigate their emotions. Many of the time, children deserve to be able to do things that can trigger some emotions in us, but in those instances, we need to parent through these triggers.

Why Is Recognizing Your Triggers Important?

Many of the experts say that there is unresolved trauma that can be passed through generations and continue to plague our kids for a long time. Once you are aware of your triggers, you increase the chances of favouring a positive response to your child's behaviour. What if there are some areas where your unintended, irrational reactions are damaging your child? Then you can start working to resolve these situations. Most of the time, you need to take a step back and analyse the situation before reacting. It will only help you recognize your triggers, and you will react more proactively.

If you start taking significant steps to identify your parenting triggers, you will uncover the roots of your past emotional wounds that are affecting your and your child's relationship. If you understand your triggering points, then you will be able to create a safe and nurturing environment for your child.

How to Identify Your Parenting Triggers?

We all have our own demons, that's for sure. But once you start your journey of getting to know and understanding your triggers, you truly start healing, emotionally and mentally. The key factor in identifying your parenting triggers is to pay attention to your feelings and look for patterns in your reactions.

The 7 clues to identifying parenting triggers are:

- *Whenever you feel extremely angry, like yelling, seeing red, or vein pooping, that means you have been triggered.*
- *When you feel sad, upset, or hurt after something your child has said or done to you (that you*

shouldn't take personally), it means you have been triggered.

- *If you are upset, angry or fearful, just out of proportion, which you realise once you are calm, you've probably been triggered.*

- *Any time you feel like everything is out of control, you are triggered.*

- *If you feel like you have experienced this kind of feeling many times before and it feels similar, it means you have certainly been triggered.*

- *If you were calm a minute ago and suddenly feel uncontrollable anger inside, you've been triggered.*

- *If you find yourself suddenly wanting to grab, punish, spank, or physically hurt your child, you have been triggered.*

How do we deal with parenting triggers?

1.   *Ask Yourself: Why am I getting triggered?*

If you are reacting aggressively, taking things personally in a situation, then it means you are not reacting towards the situation happening in front of you, but you might be reacting to something that has happened in the past and has been evoked.

When you feel such emotions triggering, start meditation and pay attention to the sensations, visual images, words, or thoughts to decipher the real meaning behind these parenting triggers. These things will help you to understand where you are coming from and how to work on them.

2. *Start Working on It.*
Once you are aware of your past hurts and emotional baggage that is currently affecting your reaction to your child, it's time to work on it. Keep a list of the situations when you responded aggressively; they could be a possible trigger. This will help you understand the events better, and you can process them thoroughly once you are calm.

Factors that may have caused anxiety, anger, stress, or insecurity can be re-understood. Working on your past experiences and letting them go and moving on is a huge step.

3. *Change is for the better.*

Since you have understood and identified your parenting triggers, it's now time to work on the change. First thing first, start imaging the probable outcomes of the situations that can be different. Focus on how these different responses make you feel. Be aware of your body language, the tone of your voice, and the words you are using while in the situation.

4.   *Start small.*

You don't need to go all in to change yourself. Start with small changes. Doing it all at once will overwhelm you and it will be hard to tackle. You can start with one thing at a time, such as: what can be done differently next time the situation arises?

Focus on the unmet needs. Our needs being met should not affect our relationship with our children.

5.   *Work on Healing.*
You need to let go of the shame and guilt caused by the trigger to start healing. Blaming yourself for your actions is not going to do any good to you or your child. Instead, practise self-compassion and empathy. You need to remind yourself that these are the things that will challenge you and that they are perfect learning and growth opportunities for you.
You need to at least try to be kind to yourself as you are to your children. Because you need this kindness to grow as a parent. Empathizing with ourselves does not mean not holding ourselves to high standards and

aiming for growth, but it means recognizing that what we are doing is hard work and it matters. You need to focus on your improvement and what your child deserves.

6. *Take your time.*
Whenever you find yourself in a situation where you feel triggered, take a moment to slow down and relax. Sometimes we feel parenting is urgent, but almost always it is not. You can simply be honest and say, "I am finding it hard; can I take a minute please?"
Taking a step back and giving yourself some space to breathe will help you handle the situation more calmly. Being gentle with yourself and granting some space will help you process the triggers. I know it will be

hard to accept and change yourself, but believe me, it's all worth it.

7.   *Accept your mistakes and apologise to your child.*
Another impactful thing you can do while working on your triggers is to be honest with your children about them. You don't have to give much detail about your triggers to them, but letting our children know about our struggles with finding certain things difficult and that it's not their fault is helpful. This helps them with empathy as well as keeps them in the loop when you are dealing with parenting triggers and you need some space or time to process them.

Also, having a parental tantrum gives you the perfect opportunity to teach your child the art of a well-formed apology. You need to make it sincere and direct. Take full responsibility for your behaviour and make it clear to them that you will take active steps to work on your behaviour in the future. You can say something like, "Hey, I am sorry for yelling at you like that when you spilled the milk. I was overreacting and I am sure I made you feel horrible. It is hard for me to handle the mess. Still, it was not OK for me to yell like that, and I am going to work on remaining calm and talking more constructively in the future. "

8. *Understand childhood development.*
It is important to be aware of your child's development at a given age to know what is reasonable and appropriate to expect from them.

Being aware of the information will help you adjust your expectations and prepare you for the behaviours that might trigger-induce you.

9. *Seek help.*

If you find yourself constantly angry and have trouble controlling it, then finding a mental health professional may be the most important option for you. You can't always manage or change things on your own. Triggers from your past relationships, childhood trauma, anxiety, or depression can be too difficult to change without support.

10. *Surround yourself with support.*

Having like-minded and supportive friends who are themselves parents is essential in the parenting journey.

Being surrounded by people who understand and who encourage you in this process is very helpful. Some might become nurturing figures for us. It is important to not feel alone on this journey and to have people who value what you are doing and value children the way you do. We aren't supposed to do this alone, and having a network that shares this lifestyle is very powerful.

With time, you will be able to analyse your triggering situations and be able to intervene before you react with anger.

Even if you do get triggered, all is not lost! Give yourself some time out, take a deep breath, and think it through.

Remember, parenting is all about learning and growing. The more you learn, the better choices you will make next time!

Chapter 4

The Number One Way to End Power Struggles - and It Works EVERY Time

There is only one thing that can truly work, every time, without fail. I know, a big call right? But honestly, there's no way for it NOT to work.

So, what's the one way to end power struggles for good?

STOP STRUGGLING FOR POWER

That's it!!!

Stop struggling for power!

You can't struggle for power against yourself. If you stop trying to overpower your children then there can't be any power struggles.

Power and control are actually not essential elements to the parent-child relationship. Seriously! You can ditch both of them right now. Exchange them for more peace, cooperation, and mutual respect in your home. Here's how...

Change your perspective

"We might say it's our job to be "in control," in the sense of creating a healthy and safe environment, offering guidance, and setting limits—but it's not our job to be "controlling," in the sense of demanding absolute obedience or relying on pressure or continuous regulation. In fact, although it may sound paradoxical, we need to be in control of helping them to gain control over their own lives. The goal is empowerment rather than conformity, and the methods are respectful rather than coercive." -Alfie Kohn

Mainstream parenting is based on a control and power dynamic. Parents are often told it is their job to control their children, to force them to 'behave', and to 'teach them a lesson'. But think about it... healthy relationships don't work that way, do they? We are told that parent-child relationships are a prototype for all future relationships, so we really should consider what we're modelling.

In no other relationship would the same level of control be endorsed. In no other area of life would unthinking obedience be praised. Children are people, like anyone else. The rules don't change because of age. This kind of relationship surely has the same negative effects on children as it does on adults.

"We're unlikely to meet our long-term goals for our kids unless we're ready to ask the following question: Is it possible that what I just did with them had more to do with my needs, my fears, and my own upbringing than with what's really in their best interests?" -Alfie Kohn

Luckily, there is a better, more peaceful, more respectful way to relate to children. It requires moving from a 'doing to' perspective of parenting to a 'working with' mindset. You're not trying to control your child, you're trying to connect with them and live together peacefully. You strive to communicate authentically in a way that allows everyone to get their needs met, instead of simply (and ineffectively) trying to control another person so they do what you want.

I appreciate that this might be a really challenging concept! Especially if you've always been led to believe that children are untrustworthy, incapable, and needing adult control. You might instantly fear bringing to life the old saying 'give an inch and they'll take a mile'. Images of your child morphing into your own little Veruca Salt might be running through your head. I encourage you to question your assumptions about children, and where they originated from.

In the end, no one can make another person do anything, and making parenting a fight cancels out much of the enjoyment. The truth is, parenting is not about control, but connection. Work on that and you will need no special techniques for 'power struggles'.

"The level of cooperation parents get from their children is usually equal to the level of connection children feel with their parents." – Pam Leo

Hopefully you're willing to make some changes and your mind is open to thinking about children in a different way. But what do you actually do? How do you stop struggling for power?

Give up these things:

1.Control

"The dominant problem with parenting in our society isn't permissiveness, but the fear of permissiveness. We're so worried about spoiling kids that we often end up overcontrolling them." -Alfie Kohn

In our society, we rationalise the use of unnecessary control over children by telling ourselves that it's 'for their own good'. Because they are younger and less experienced we think that justifies treating them as inferior

Children deserve to be treated with no less respect than adults, but it's so ingrained that it's really hard to overcome, or even recognise all the little ways that childism seeps into everyday life.

2. Punishment

"Where did we ever get the crazy idea that in order to make children do better, first we have to make them feel worse? Think of the last time you felt humiliated or treated unfairly. Did you feel like cooperating or doing better?" – Jane Nelsen

Punishment is obviously a form of control, but I thought it deserved a specific mention. It does not make sense, and it does not work.

"Misbehavior and punishment are not opposites that cancel each other – on the contrary they breed and reinforce each other." – Haim G. Ginott

Punishment doesn't make a child less likely not to do the same thing in the future, it just means they'll work on being better at not getting caught. It's also contrary to the goal of fostering connection with children.

3. Rewards

"The problem is that rewards and punishments are really just two sides

While rewards may seem 'nicer', the goal is still control. Rewards, bribes, and praise have also been shown to be ineffective and counterproductive. Rewards are unnecessary. If you're grateful for something your child has done, just thank them authentically!

4. Demands

"My children gave me some invaluable lessons about demands. Somehow I had gotten it into my head that, as a parent, my job was to make

demands. I learned, however, that I could make all the demands in the world but still couldn't make my children do anything. This is a humbling lesson in power for those of us who believe that, because we're a parent, teacher, or manager, our job is to change other people and make them behave. Here were these youngsters letting me know that I couldn't make them do anything. All I could do was make them wish they had—through punishment. Then eventually they taught me that any time I was foolish enough to make them wish they had complied by punishing them, they had ways of making me wish that I hadn't!"
-Marshall Rosenberg

It's quite shocking when you take notice of how people generally speak to children. There is so much micromanaging and demanding, is it any wonder children are fighting for some control over their own lives? Children naturally resist control, and that is a good thing! Move from making demands to requests that children have a choice in, as much as possible! The key to telling the difference is knowing that you are happy for them to reply with either 'yes' or 'no'. A respectful relationship is not demanding.

"When people hear demands, it looks to them as though our caring and respect and love are conditional. It looks as though we are only going to

care for them as people when they do what we want." -Marshall Rosenberg

What do I do instead?

Move towards respectful parenting and live in partnership with your children instead of as adversaries! You can read more about what respectful parenting is here, but here are some things to start with...

- **Build Connection**

"Unless we understand the potential for connection in each moment of each day, we will miss countless wonderful windows of opportunity for interaction with our children." -Shefali Tsabary,

I can't emphasise this enough... Connection is the key. Punitive, coercive parenting breaks connection which means children are less likely to listen to you or be interested in working things out together! Make it your mission to replace correction with connection and you'll notice a huge difference.

- **Empathize**

"Empathy is when a person accurately communicates that they see another's intentions and emotional state. It means watching our child's frustration and focusing on how life feels in that little child's body, while putting our own anger and

Children have a LOT of feelings, and our job is to help support them so they grow up to be adults who are equipped to recognise and regulate their emotions. Oftentimes, we haven't experienced a lot of empathy ourselves and so we struggle with the feelings of others. But, as I have said before "every time you dismiss or minimize your child's feelings, you actually make your job harder. You very rarely succeed at making them stop anyway, and it's more likely that they will need more support from you in the future rather than less. If you don't hear the message they are trying to send you, the messenger just gets louder and louder until you do. Children are looking for empathy and understanding. If they don't get it, they'll keep trying."

Whenever you feel the urge to control, turn to empathy instead.

• Radiate Acceptance

Parents with radical acceptance! Let go of preconceived ideas of how children 'should' behave, and instead respond to them moment by moment. Understand and accept them for the unique and wonderful individuals that they are instead of trying to change them.

• Problem solve

When you encounter problems or disagreements, work together to find a solution instead of 'laying down the law'. When I say that we parent without control, people often wonder what that looks like. Read more about what we do instead here.

• **Focus on YOUR Boundaries**

"Conventional parenting experts claim that children feel more secure when their parents regularly "set limits," which means making rules and establishing "consequences"

But this approach fails to distinguish arbitrary controls from real limitations and authentic boundaries. Life naturally provides plenty of limits without you adding to them.

Parents are supposed to empower their children, not limit them." -Scott Noelle

Parents are often advised to 'set limits' with their kids, but this again puts the focus on 'doing to' instead of 'working with'. Remember, you can't actually make anyone do what you want so it makes more sense to instead focus on protecting your own personal boundaries. This is a great read which explains this concept more fully.

- **Model Graciousness**

"Children do not learn from what we say. They don't even learn from what we do. They learn from who we are.

And they're always watching." –Visible Child

What do you do when children just refuse to cooperate when you really need them to? Model graciousness. Model what you want to see and trust that you are enough. This post is an absolute must read.

- **Communicate Effectively**

Most of us don't even know how to identify our feelings and needs, let alone communicate them in an appropriate way. This takes some work, but when you get it, things change dramatically. And, you're empowering the next generation to grow up with greater emotional literacy.

"Behind intimidating messages are merely people appealing to us to meet their needs. A difficult message becomes an opportunity to enrich someone's life." -Marshall Rosenberg

All of these things will make a huge difference in moving away from power struggles, towards more respectful and connected parenting.

But here's the catch...

These are not 'techniques' to use on your children.

This is a perspective shift and means coming to a new understanding and view of your relationship. Respectful parenting is not something you can 'use sometimes', and the goal isn't what 'works' to ultimately get your way and have your children do what you want.

It's about being equal. No one has power over anyone else. Just as you don't control your children, they don't control you. It doesn't mean letting them 'do whatever they want' at the expense of your needs and personal boundaries. It means making considered choices and honouring their freedom and autonomy as much as possible. It means doing some internal work and challenging assumptions and 'the way it's always been done'.

So if you really want to end battles and power struggles...simply stop struggling for power.

It's not a quick fix, but it's immensely worth it. When you experience a mutually respectful relationship with your child, and the connection and joy that follows, there is no turning back.

Chapter 5

These 9 child-building up tips can help you feel more fulfilled as a parent.

1. Boost Your Child's Self-Esteem

Kids start developing their sense of self as babies when they see themselves through their parents' eyes. Your tone of voice, your body language, and your every expression are absorbed by your kids. Your words and actions as a parent affect their developing self-esteem more than anything else.

Praising accomplishments, however small, will make them feel proud; letting kids do things independently will make them feel capable and strong. By contrast, belittling comments or comparing a child unfavorably with another will make kids feel worthless.

Avoid making loaded statements or using words as weapons. Comments like "What a stupid thing to do!" or "You act more like a baby than your little brother!" cause damage just as physical blows do.

Choose your words carefully and be compassionate. Let your kids know that everyone makes mistakes and that you still love them, even when you don't love their behavior.

2. Catch Kids Being Good

Have you ever stopped to think about how many times you react negatively to your kids in a given day? You may find yourself criticizing far more often than complimenting. How would you feel about a boss who treated you with that much negative guidance, even if it was well-intentioned?

The more effective approach is to catch kids doing something right: "You made your bed without being asked — that's terrific!" or "I was watching you play with your sister and you were very patient." These statements will do more to encourage good behavior over the long run than repeated scoldings.

Make a point of finding something to praise every day. Be generous with rewards — your love, hugs, and compliments can work wonders and are often rewarded enough. Soon you will find you are "growing" more of the behavior you would like to see.

3. Set Limits and Be Consistent With Your Discipline

Discipline is necessary in every household. The goal of discipline is to help kids choose acceptable behaviors and learn self-control. They may test the limits you establish for them, but they need those limits to grow into responsible adults.

Establishing house rules helps kids understand your expectations and develop self-control. Some rules might include: no TV until homework is done, and no hitting, name-calling, or hurtful teasing allowed.

You might want to have a system in place: one warning, followed by consequences such as a "time out" or loss of privileges. A common mistake parents make is failure to follow through with the consequences. You can't discipline kids for talking back one day and ignore it the next. Being consistent teaches what you expect.

4. Make Time for Your Kids

It's often hard for parents and kids to get together for a family meal, let alone spend quality time together. But there is probably nothing kids would like more. Get up 10 minutes earlier in the morning so you can eat breakfast with your child or leave the dishes in the sink and take a walk after dinner. Kids who aren't getting the attention they want from their parents often act out or misbehave because they're sure to be noticed that way.

Many parents find it rewarding to schedule together time with their kids. Create a "special night" each week to be together and let your kids help decide how to spend the time. Look for other ways to connect — put a note or something special in your kid's lunchbox.

Teens seem to need less undivided attention from their parents than younger kids. Because there are fewer windows of opportunity for parents and teens to get together, parents should do their best to be available when their teen does express a desire to talk or participate in family activities. Attending concerts, games, and other events with your teen communicates caring and lets you get to know more about your child and his or her friends in important ways.

Don't feel guilty if you're a working parent. It is the many little things you do — making popcorn, playing cards, window shopping — that kids will remember.

5. Be a Good Role Model

Young kids learn a lot about how to act by watching their parents. The younger they are, the more cues they take from you. Before you lash out or blow your top in front of your child, think about this: Is that how you want your child to behave when angry? Be aware that you're constantly being watched by your kids. Studies have shown that children who hit usually have a role model for aggression at home.

Model the traits you wish to see in your kids: respect, friendliness, honesty, kindness, tolerance. Exhibit unselfish behavior. Do things for other people without expecting a reward. Express thanks and offer compliments. Above all, treat your kids the way you expect other people to treat you.

6. Make Communication a Priority

You can't expect kids to do everything simply because you, as a parent, "say so." They want and deserve explanations as much as adults do. If we don't take time to explain, kids will begin to wonder about our values and motives and whether they have any basis. Parents who reason with their kids allow them to understand and learn in a nonjudgmental way.

Make your expectations clear. If there is a problem, describe it, express your feelings, and invite your child to work on a solution with you. Be sure to include consequences. Make suggestions and offer choices. Be open to your child's suggestions as well. Negotiate. Kids who participate in decisions are more motivated to carry them out.

7. Be Flexible and Willing to Adjust Your Parenting Style

If you often feel "let down" by your child's behavior, perhaps you have unrealistic expectations. Parents who think in "shoulds" (for example, "My kid should be potty-trained by now") might find it helpful to read up on the matter or to talk to other parents or child development specialists.

Kids' environments have an effect on their behavior, so you might be able to change that behavior by changing the environment. If you find yourself constantly saying "no" to your 2-year-old, look for ways to alter your surroundings so that fewer things are off-limits. This will cause less frustration for both of you.

As your child changes, you'll gradually have to change your parenting style. Chances are, what works with your child now won't work as well in a year or two.

Teens tend to look less to their parents and more to their peers for role models. But continue to provide guidance, encouragement, and appropriate discipline while allowing your teen to earn more independence. And seize every available moment to make a connection!

8. Show That Your Love Is Unconditional

As a parent, you're responsible for correcting and guiding your kids. But how you express your corrective guidance makes all the difference in how a child receives it.

When you have to confront your child, avoid blaming, criticizing, or fault-finding, which hurt self-esteem and can lead to resentment. Instead, try to nurture and encourage, even when disciplining your kids. Make sure they know that although you want and expect better next time, your love is there no matter what.

9. Know Your Own Needs and Limitations as a Parent

Face it — you are an imperfect parent. You have strengths and weaknesses as a family leader. Recognize your abilities — "I am loving and dedicated." Vow to work on your weaknesses — "I need to be more consistent with discipline." Try to have realistic expectations for yourself, your partner, and your kids. You don't have to have all the answers — be forgiving of yourself.

And try to make parenting a manageable job. Focus on the areas that need the most attention rather than trying to address everything all at once. Admit it when you're burned out. Take time out from parenting to do things that will make you happy.

Focusing on your needs does not make you selfish. It simply means you care about your own well-being, which is another important value to model for your children.